EVERYONE'S GOING

POEMS ON GRIEF AND MORTALITY

GEORGE H NORTHRUP

atmosphere press

© 2025 George Northrup

Published by Atmosphere Press

Cover design by Felipe Betim

No part of this book may be reproduced without permission from the author except in brief quotations and in reviews.

Atmospherepress.com

Table of Contents

CIRCLES OF RELUCTANCE

Chair by the Window	3
Return Trip	4
The Lid	6
To the House of Your Father	7
Planting Fields Arboretum, Followed by Lunch	9
Making It Official	11
Daydream About a Mother's Daydream	12
Christmas Mourning	14
Good Friday in the Sky	16
Memorial Day	17
Your 98th Birthday	18
Extended Memory	19
Little Wooden Things	20
Trellis of Mourning	21

A SPARROW'S MEMORY

A Wife's Cancer Prayer	29
In the Woman Cave	30
Awaiting Flowers	31
No Thanksgiving	32
With This Ring	33

OPEN ARMS

A Soft Retirement	37
Dorothy's Last Year	38

One Death, a Threnody	39
The News From Culver City	40
Consanguinity at Auschwitz	41
Decision	42
Even an Attractive Cage	44
Last Haircut	45
Bedside Manners	48
Atlantic Waves	50
Into Pieces	52
Meditation on Picasso's Old Guitarist	53

DIE BEFORE YOU DIE

Accelerating	57
Throwing It All Out	58
Last Car	60
Daredevil	62
Fugaces Labuntur Anni	63
Für Elyse	64
Wary of Unbearable Lightness	66
Asymptomatic Mortality	67
Lives to Spare	68
Perish the Thought	69
Sonnet for Thich Nhat Hanh	70
Mortality Through the Seasons	71

POISED TO EVAPORATE

Heroes of the Holocene	77
Late-Stage American Hegemony	79
You Don't Need a Weatherman	82
Subject to Change Without Notice	83

CIRCLES OF RELUCTANCE

Give sorrow words; the grief that does not speak
whispers the o'er-fraught heart and bids it break.
    —William Shakespeare, *Macbeth*

Ich bin ja noch kein Wissender im Wehe[1]

    —Rainer Maria Rilke, ["Vielleicht, dass ich durch schwere Berge gehe"]

Chair by the Window

My father sleeps serenely,
soundly through the night,
even much of the day.

His appetite is good,
abiding mood content.
Legs no longer carry him.

Family, events of the day,
global calamities flicker
on the screen of awareness.

His chief preoccupation
remains as always deep décor
on the inscape of his skull.

Having accepted
the invitation,
he awaits the date.

Return Trip

Southern skies were teasing me with portents:
blue's deepest clarity, enveloping white clouds,
billowing sheets of lightning,
sudden rivers of rain, black night of course,
and even that unlikely rainbow
astride the rehabilitation center.

But all these heralded no momentous event—
only an old man, frail and thin,
eyebrows overtaking his face
with great authority as he lay in bed
whispering between the sharp
reminders of his pain.
"Do not be fooled," he said,
"by polished floors and costly doors."
He showed me his diaper,
the feeding tube that pierced his gut,
peeling lips around his now-diminished mouth,
and once, the pooling tears
that flushed his face with shame.

In the wallpaper he could see
lions devouring steers—where I saw tulips.
He instructed me how nurses should perform
the *morning care* for him, but don't.
He corrected Mother's grammar
and made a disapproving face
(perfected over all these years)

as he repeated what an aide had preached
about no pain in heaven's keep.
All as if to say,
Can this be my destination?
Another almost-ghost in fitful sleep
inside this terminal of sad delirium,
where ancient bones fade slowly
into shadows, tardy for the tomb.

Too quickly it was time for me to leave,
astonished to feel so cheerful resting
and chatting in this penultimate place.
No urge to grieve, no anxious thoughts
of what to say.

I think I faltered only once—
when I returned my rental car
to the beautiful, impatient agent,
and I, an invalid for her,
could not still the beating
of the windshield wipers
or disarm the automatic locks.

The Lid

These are my people, gathered in whispers,
a quiet cohort bending the arc
of each other's lives to this reluctant point,
drawn together in that shuddering unease
between the futile agonies
of looking back and looking forward.

They are here today, bent in capitulation,
because the beckoning lid remains open
in this mock Victorian parlor of velvet drapes,
gold painted trim, and cut glass chandeliers.
The lights above are dimmed except for one
that spots the honored guest.

Tomorrow we will close the lid,
declare an end but not achieve it, not yet.
Till then we carry the gaze of each other's eyes,
understanding too well our sorry purpose here.

And there are no words to calm this coiled grief,
nothing adequate to say—hence bromide and ritual.
Hence the nervous laugh, change of subject—
anything to escape the quiet tension
at this sad altar of satin and mahogany,
where the fragrance of flowers brings no delight,
their pastels no glimpse into beauty.

To the House of Your Father

Life is not so long, compared
to the eternity that follows.
Living tempts us more,
up to the point when death,
enticing with its balmy respite,
burgeons in appeal,
compelling as azaleas at their peak,
nearly smothering the green.

"I'm in my father's house,"
I heard you say, as if still dreaming.
Delicious death aroused your appetite
like pastry from the oven. Soon—
to mingle with bucolic forebears
in easeful anonymity.
If peace is good, then death is better.

Old age looks pensively beyond
as from the cliffs on the Amalfi coast,
finding only endless blue above, below.
Yourself a particle of dust
inviting any vagrant breeze
to lift you through the sparkling air.

At last, a little gust obliged.
Nature, sometimes tardy
representing all its keen constituents,
would nonetheless grant every dying wish.

Father, my sorrow blisters
not on your account, but mine.
On sleepless nights, my eyes look up
for one of your occasional, accepting nods.
You are only half demised,
it seems, for I still speak to you.

Teach me sotto voce if you cannot shout,
when sentimental ignorance distracts me
from your quietly convincing dialogue
with death.

Planting Fields Arboretum, Followed by Lunch

This is what an Olmstead
makes with glass and iron,
as much temple as greenhouse—
a fitting place to seek your ghost again,
amid these centenarian camellias.
But blossoms are late this year,
not ready for your birthday.
Some panes have shattered
from the weight of snow,
more ruin than reunion.

I retreat to the Maine Maid Inn,
an approximation of the world
you were born to.
There, two men on opposite ends
of the bar shout to each other:
*Guess how old Fats Domino
and Betty Hutton are today?*
And *Hey, look at that one
in the green miniskirt!*

Between soup and salad,
as I try to summon memories of you,
two televisions play at once
on different channels:
a flabbergasted Al Sharpton
responds to the revelation

that his great grandfather
was a slave owned by
Strom Thurmond's ancestor.

Let me tell you—a competing voice insists,
as if anyone might disagree—
it gets cold in North Dakota.

You wouldn't like it here, old boy.
Despite the fireplaces, wide plank floors,
it's not your cherished, rustic world at all—
so rich in history, but irretrievable today.

Making It Official

The last of my father's socks
wore out today, joining
the last of his handkerchiefs,
the last of his flannel shirts.

Some Old Spice beckons
from the bathroom vanity
to splash on my face
each Sunday morning,
as he did faithfully.

Once that is gone,
only threadbare memories
will connect us,
and the gold ring
I wear on his birthday,
but never noticed on his finger.

Daydream About a Mother's Daydream

Here I am alone in the kitchen,
ironing a linen handkerchief
while in the living room
The Ed Sullivan Show is broadcasting
that song from *Guys and Dolls*,
"I love you a bushel and a peck.
A bushel and a peck
and a hug around the neck."

Today is Mother's Day—
sweet sentiments for me
and dinner at the only restaurant
in this suffocating town
barely four streets wide.

A city girl, almost a flapper in my day,
what am I doing exiled with a husband
more devoted to his tractor and pitchfork?
Unspeakable, I know—I should be
grateful for the honors of the day.

My first born put to rest at 21,
two other babes evicted early
from my womb. (He always frowns
and says I shouldn't count them.)

Now even the youngest pulls away
into a man's life.

He will carry this handkerchief,
white flag of my surrender.

I've been standing over ironing boards
since I was 12, my own mother too frail,
and I the eldest of five.
She gave it all up in her sixties.

Ten years to go.
How many handkerchiefs is that?

Christmas Mourning

En route, a sudden storm
scattered flurries in the way.
And now—this eerie stillness
in the frozen air preparing gifts
of snow and death for Christmas.

Breakfast conversation
ventures politics and markets.
Unspoken is the thought,
No call yet from the hospital?
She must have lived the night.

Oblivious, Buster the cat,
with fur of silky cinnamon,
plays willing jester
to our willing disbelief.
The eldest grandson pleads,
"Why give up now, at 92?"

We recognize the season's tune
but cannot carry it
as Margaret hangs
upon the door of death
like some macabre wreath.

The ventilator sounds an alien hiss
as morphine drips into her blood.

Circles of Reluctance

Wild heartbeats in the hush of night
drum the final vigil,
summon tremulous descendants.

Good Friday in the Sky

Flight 7233 lifts off at three o'clock.
Fulgent sunlight inundates
the atmosphere, sparkling the sea.
And here I am between,
hanging in the air,
wings and fuselage a cross
upon this Calvary of azure sky.

Ascending in this way,
scourges of the earth sink far below—
a liberation much like death.
With everything subtracted,
emptiness consumes the troubled mind.
I sit in safety on the upper air:
no danger where there is no fear.

Sister and brother wait
on an island off the Carolina coast,
our first attempt to celebrate
since we shivered at the grave.
Live oaks and Spanish moss,
crab cakes, hush puppies,
and a lance into the side.

Memorial Day

I would have told you gladly
how I spent today in the garden:
the weeds I pulled, lilies of the valley
I transplanted by the pond,
some forgotten amaryllis bulbs
I potted, hoping for the best.

I would have told you
all about the frogs I startled
with the garden hose,
beacon silver set among the rocks,
and tongue depressors
marking homes of future daffodils.

You would have told me
that you never had a green thumb,
and so you loved the flowers
I would bring in spring and summer,
flowers I would send at Christmastime.

I would have told you gladly.
You would have heard me gladly,
your old heart beating faster,
needing nothing more
than my voice reporting flowers.

Your 98th Birthday

"Sie herbsten den Wein ihrer Augen."[2]
—Paul Celan, *Die Winzer*

A heavy rain assails the awning
here at Koenig's Restaurant,
bustling wind the only traffic in the street.
Stepping out tonight demands a reason.

The waiter here does not remember me
from last October's birthday meal.
I choose the Kassler Rippchen—
too much food, and I without an appetite.

Not long before the end,
your gastroenterologist insisted
on a colonoscopy, one of many tests
to solve the puzzle of your falling weight.

To me your eyes confided this—
the final harvest of a widow's grief,
tired fruit detaching from the vine,
juices dripping from the grapes.

Extended Memory

I remember everything
about this little gardenia bush,
how the buds of your eyes blossomed
when I surprised you with it,
the wilted look on your face
when you gave it back
a few months later, worried
you would kill the helpless plant,
trusting me to keep it alive.
That was twenty years ago.

I remember the time I asked my wife
to water it while I attended
a conference in Rome.
She did what you might have—
inclined to be too nurturing—
and half was drowned.
Now the surviving half
grows to one side like a trained bonsai,
wintering in the greenhouse,
summering on the front steps,
where it flowers like that first time
in your arms.

I considered repotting my gardenia,
tilted upright to look less like an amputee.
But I have come to prefer this injured way,
holding all that was perishable between us.

Little Wooden Things

I found these little wooden things
in a cracked plastic case
with his nail clippers and jackknife.
One of them rattles like a Mexican jumping bean;
the other resembles an elongated acorn.
Souvenirs or artifacts, their provenance
obscure—what did they mean to him?

I know I can't keep everything.
I've thrown away her final apron, barely used,
and an ugly polyester tablecloth
I wouldn't want to picture in their dining room.
All these cherished boxes should be
headed for the trash, the attic at least,
but I have kept them twenty years,
stacked in the corner of a bedroom.

Grief walks in circles of reluctance.
So I replace these little wooden things
next to his nail clippers, tucked into
a larger box with photographs,
some of her needlework,
one volume of a 1930's stamp collection.
A son of mine may find these heirlooms
on a snowy afternoon like this,
and with a fond detachment, let them go.

Trellis of Mourning

I

When I was eight, Richard,
and you began slow death
from Hodgkin's disease,
my emotions dangled helplessly
like slaughtered cows on hooks,
my timid questions quarantined
inside a child's skull.

If anyone at home had known
how to catch grief like a basketball
and bounce it down the court,
I might have run into the game.
But your dying circled like a satellite,
cold and far—no one I knew
could reach you, stranded there.

In the pantry was a button jar,
at the bottom of the cellar stairs
a burlap bag for rags.
In a house of treasures to recycle,
couldn't we, when I was ten,
have found a place for you?

II

Luis in California,
Zeke in New York, while driving home

haben ins Schwarze getroffen.[3]
This aberrant partnership of youth
and death twisted grief beyond expression,
toward a path without direction.
I sponsored planting of a tree in Israel.
I sold my Chrysler, rode the IRT.

In the lilac light of spring, Hussein,
you spun a bullet through your head.
Squirming in your pain I gathered mine,
awkwardly at first, trying to clear my eyes.
Through haunted silence
I gaped into a ragged night,
woke to a ruby-fisted dawn.
Slowly I climbed the trellis of this mourning.
From you I learned—as grief cuts deeper into life—
the prospect of a sharply-scented peace.

After you were born, Daniel,
silent tumors hidden in your baby brain,
I stumbled in the harness of my sorrow,
which you, in antic motion, did not share.
In time your nimble stride persuaded me—
your passage through this shattered life
as a ghost through a wall, to all appearances
content with our calamity.

Ever since Barry's hip replacement,
Kumar's heart attack, and Ronald's diabetes—
the message of mortality made dying

so routine that when they diagnosed you,
Bert, with pancreatic cancer,
we both could look away, unmoved.
You researched novel treatments in Japan.

Afraid to break
my wishful covenant with death,
I wanted to instill each morning
with a pious chant: pretium magnum
sensilis vitae et propinquitas mortis,[4]
as if grief might disappear in poetry
or be grafted on a branch of equanimity.

III

Held back by fear
or buried in the tasks of living,
grief is a white tiger locked in a trunk
and sealed with strips of tape,
left in the back of the garage.
(Your grief was like that, Mother.)
Sometimes the lettering on the tape says
She's in heaven now
It's all for the best
Try to be strong
You still have other children
He lived a full life
God has a plan—
all the specious consolations
cloaked in hopes of comfort.

Of course you wouldn't dare inspect this trunk,
nor walk too close to where the tiger growls.
In time you avoid the garage completely
and even the adjacent kitchen door.

After the adhesive dries out,
the tape begins to wrinkle and crack,
and the white tiger (still pacing in this cage)
has never accepted confinement,
has not grown less dreadful
during the long delay,
has only one thing in its mind,
only one message to deliver,
sniffing for opportunity.

That day when the lid flies open—
too late in the leaping moment
you realize the clarity of tooth and claw.
It would have been easier
in the first place, all those years ago,
to have offered the tiger an arm,
a leg, even the whole body—
whatever it wanted, losing nothing
in complete surrender—

instead of all the trepidation,
all the nightmares,
all the moods that drifted in
as if from nowhere,
and the anxious, weary passage
of so many empty years.

IV

The two of you, Mother and Father,
accepted the congested heart
and merciful pneumonia
after almost a century sturdy and wise—
the last few years slipping slowly,
gently to the end—final flourish
of a long, inexorable oration
building to its one conclusion.

After the last climactic breath,
there was only the wordless gasping
and the piercing, cankered knowledge
of the end—but now without aversion.

Today was your wedding anniversary.
The two of you and I
and a gleaming white tiger
met for lunch, ate goulash and strudel,
and wept in Victor Koenig's Restaurant.

A SPARROW'S MEMORY

I come to a place
where nothing shines, ever.
>—Dante, Inferno, Canto 4, line 151[5]

This is the Hour of Lead—
Remembered, if outlived,
As Freezing persons, recollect the Snow—
First—Chill—then Stupor—then the letting go—
>—Emily Dickinson #341

A Wife's Cancer Prayer

Let the radiation begin.
Let someone hear me when I fall.
Let my sister arrive,
her tears their own beseeching.

Let me hold the spoon without tremor.
Let my bowels remember
the patient work of peristalsis.
Let my decline lift all compassion.

Let there be oxygen tanks.
Let it be time for the next Dilaudid.
Let me inhabit a world more spacious
than this bed, cradle of my anguish.

Let me leave the others softly as I sleep.

In the Woman Cave

It was her turf, and I respected that,
even after she gave up cooking.
Now I—the new chef—wonder where
her ghost concealed the measuring spoons.

I parted with children's birthday candles,
an ancient bottle of molasses,
expired pancake mix forgotten
in the back of a high cupboard.

Such surfeit here of goblet, dish, pan,
and silverware, even for a busy holiday—
but especially for a solitary widower
just learning how, one eye on the hourglass.

Awaiting Flowers

With age, she wanted waist-high garden beds,
had a trio of them built with cinder block
and brick, secure enough to last for centuries.

She would never rush the season,
sometimes planting tomatoes in July,
and far too tolerant of weeds, I thought,
as I banished uninvited guests.

Now she is planted in the ground herself,
never again to climb like a vine above her roots.
Memory preserves her here, in the soil
where her fingers took the harvest.

Three sarcophagi have waited in full sun,
in the temperance of spring, for signs of life.
This year I test the sprinklers, add fresh compost,
nurture flowers instead of vegetables
in a half-hearted plan for growing
new meanings to convalesce the old.

No Thanksgiving

For years she scattered birdseed
on the front steps, at first in winter,
and then, because she could not help herself,
year-round—sometimes twice a day.

Cancer treatments interfered;
death stopped her hand completely.

Long after what I would have guessed
to be the limits of a sparrow's memory,
three of them landed on the steps today,
bobbing their heads in consternation.

With This Ring

Still dripping from the shower,
I give this wedding band a tug,
surprised I can remove it now
after so many failed attempts.

Locked in place for decades
by swollen fat cells nourished
in a lengthy marriage, the ring
has visibly denied this widowhood.

My plan to part with it
relied upon the daily discipline
of giving up molecule by molecule
everything gained since the wedding.

Now, here it is—a suddenly empty
loop of gold in my palm,
leaving an indelible tattoo
in the finger's dented flesh.

OPEN ARMS

I had not thought death had undone so many.
    —T. S. Eliot, *The Waste Land*

This quiet Dust was Gentlemen and Ladies.
    —Emily Dickinson #813

A Soft Retirement

I remember Dolores, childless aunt
inviting nieces and nephews to the farm
all those years ago—a world of candled eggs,
red cabbages, potatoes, and a farmer's
deep concern for all things in the ground.
After we grew up and settled far away,
you and Eddie sold the farm,
exchanged hard work for soft retirement.
The door to Florida was open, and you went.

Well water with a sulfurous smell,
the yellow barn, and popcorn strung around the tree
passed on decades ago except in living memory,
long before your swift surrender to intensive care,
antique organs eager for a ghoulish trophy.

Even in Florida summer slips away.
I feel as if I dig your grave today,
shoveling this heavy snow in New York
while you turn cold in Naples,
approaching your beloved soil.
Remembering the northern winter,
wise in the ways that seasons should be spent—
you saw the door was open, and you went.

Dorothy's Last Year

Up until death, the future is a trick
played incrementally.
She never planned to linger long,
so frail after burying Tom.
She counted things to cherish still,
accepting the decline.
Growing older, deeper in the past,
she needed nothing more invented,
no new music or ideas.
She inhabited the world she knew
even as it disappeared.

Her death exploding in his cells,
my old friend shudders,
now an orphan child.
After all the false alarms,
he no longer fears impending grief
outside an old stone church
under a puffy gray sky
in a quiet town at winter's end.

This minister is kindly, not a fool,
repeats the off-white lies
about death's triumph in the sky.
He could have said,
"There are bad deaths and good;
this one good, like on Good Friday."
He could have said, "In any death—
the mirror of our own mortality."

One Death, a Threnody

There was only one death
when Rob lay dying, fingering the dial,
emptying the room with sudden silence.
Only one death when Rob drifted out
on the last of his own weary breath.

There is only one death for all the dying,
one rosy pyre for all the little fears.
Only one death, beyond denying,
after courages and tears.

There was only one death as my friend,
Claire, flew home from that Pacific shore,
remembering the day when Rob was four.
Only one death, but the living keep trying,
always trying, for fewer or for more.

The News From Culver City

What silence gathers in the dark?
What myopic vision scans the night?
What searching looks we give ourselves
still gathered near the telephone.

Why think just now about her eyes
(like birds'), her slippers, and her robe,
her careful hair, her kitchen and
her corned beef sandwiches?

Tomorrow will the sunlight fall
too full, too brightly on the day?
And will the air seem too composed
as if admonished not to stir?

I fall into a heavy sleep and dream
of insect wings—just wings—
that flutter softly to the ground,
their bodies so conspicuously vanished.

Consanguinity at Auschwitz

She lights a candle,
sterilizes the needle,
pricks the ball
of her left thumb,
drawing blood
she rubs on the wall
of a ruined crematorium.

She had to do it,
to reconnect
the severed bloodlines.
But she worries
that her grandmother,
(huddled there in 1944
with the four youngest siblings
of her father, a survivor)
would shudder in dismay
at the shedding
of even one more
drop of Jewish blood.

Decision

Only seventeen, he had endured enough,
stranded in hollow pain—
staring sleepless at the pitch of night,
each succeeding day unraveling
his mended hopes.

He stopped home after school
to empty his wallet,
except for the card
that would identify him.
Then, on to the platform—
the stage, almost—where,
any minute, an express train
would thunder across his future.

It would leave him in its wake,
mangled corpse of sorry flesh,
simultaneously killing off
any second thoughts, any kisses
or guitars, any teenagers of his own.

He had never heard that shocking claim,
"We had to destroy the village
in order to save it,"
but had lived long enough
to understand the savage urge
to seek relief through violence,
to hope for salvage in ruin.

He would launch himself like a rocket
into the infinite mercy of death.
As the train approached,
he leaned toward the tracks
and stared at the iron face
of his executioner.
Last legs tense, amazed
by the shakes that overtook him:
an inner, opposing force
roaring its own, insistent message.
Fear, then terror, tightened in his chest.

For weeks, everything had plunged
in value except this one ambition.
Now it, too, fizzled into failure,
joining the queasy rumble
of quandary and regret.

"Mom, I need help," he texted.
An ambulance hurried him
to the Department of Emergencies
for a surreal weekend, locked
in a ward of unbelonging.
He accepted the Lithium that was offered,
and for a while no one could say what,
exactly, had changed everything—
a drug known for occasional miracles
or the unblinking headlights
of a ruthless commuter train.

Even an Attractive Cage

"I cannot guarantee to endure at all the confinements of even an attractive cage."
>—Amelia Earhart, in a letter to her husband on their wedding day in 1931.

Every binding contract chafes.
Even loving arms restrict
your urgent need to fly.
Revered, familiar roles impose
tradition's veils
and stifling precedents.

Your inner Lilith calls,
seduces with her conjured visions
of the radically new:
ad astra per aspera,[6]
ambition escalating open mind to open sky.

Instead, a box of death awaits,
dungeon of the *mare liberum*.[7]
No buoyant courage struts
in that lugubrious infinity.
So freedom climbs, and gravity
extends its open arms.

Last Haircut

They let you in OK?

I always get looks from the nurses.
I tell them I'm your sister—
don't know if they believe me.
Who sent the flowers?

Friends of Mom.

I gotta take this shoe off, it's killing me.
So what's going on here?

Death... How's work?

It's getting too cold to dress like this—
what can I do? You need a haircut!

A haircut? You make me laugh.
Do you ever think about the future?

Sure, I'll screw some guy from Pittsburgh,
and he'll set me up in his pied-à-terre.
Then we'll get married, have three kids.
The oldest goes to Harvard, gets elected President.
The other two run Microsoft and Wal-Mart.

No, really.

Everyone's Going

I got no future. I'm like you,
only still walking the streets.

They think about a week, ten days at most.

That's nice. I mean—not to drag it out.
Me, I would die fast, like from bad dope
or some psycho cuts my throat.
Not from something nobody ever heard of.
I can't stand your hair like this.
I'll send my friend up—she used to work in a salon.

For what? My hair is dying, too.

I got a scissors in my purse.
Legally it's not a weapon
if they pick you up.
Maybe I could trim it myself.
Here, let me cut a little in the front.

The wastebasket's over there.

That's it.
I better let my friend do the rest.

*Are you going to walk around with it
in your hand like that?*

Shut up. I'm going to put it in a baggie
if you must know.

My sister, the sentimental one.

If you make me cry, I'll finish you off now
with the scissors—I swear I will.

OK, OK. You don't have to settle
for a lock of my hair.
You're in my will.
It isn't much, I know—

You're a prince, but—how can I say this?
Money from men, it all feels the same.
Don't tell Mom you saw me.
Say you don't know where I am.

What if she asks about my haircut?

I don't know.
Tell her they need it for your DNA.
What are you smiling at?

I'm taking a last look at my kid sister.

Listen, I better go. Time is money.
You'll be all right.

I'll be dead all right.

Bedside Manners

From the oncologist's shocked expression
she knew she had asked the right question,
the one he dared not answer.

As he reached for words
to steady the moment—
promising research underway,
the advantages of early detection—
she knew he was leading her
into the zone of his own safety,
inviting her not to contemplate
the prowling future.

She repeated the question,
and he fell back on other bright evasions—
we will do our very best,
no one can predict with certainty—
but she fixed him
in her narrowed eyes until he felt
like a specimen under her microscope,
exposed by her scrutiny,
defenseless in this close examination.

So when she asked him a third time,
his tongue forgot all science
and the healer's optimistic watchwords.
His head began to shake,
eyes looked away, trembling lips
wordlessly confessed the answer.

A white coat stammering syllables,
he offered her the shame
of having nothing to offer
except himself as the vessel
for their collapsing hopes.

And she thanked him for that.

Atlantic Waves

In the health club
several patrons watched
with curiosity the ancient man
in daily, wordless exercise—
biceps, triceps, deltoids, pectorals—
that odd expression on his face,
some secret pleasure
seldom seen in one his age.

He, on the birthday morning,
hurried past the headlines,
studied carefully the timing
of the tides,
glanced once around the room.

Down at the marina
where all was milky glare,
no one thought too much
about an old man's purchase
of a tired rowboat on this busy,
cloudless day, a perfect day
for boating of all kinds.

No one at all observed him, smiling,
eyes lifted to beckoning blue.
He rowed and rowed,
becoming more bemused:
sand, wave, sky, wind,
bathed in light
impossible to capture.

Someone like a captain
in his proud, last heart
watched without regret
the slow receding shore.

Into Pieces

First day of spring,
seventy-two degrees,
and motorcycle boys
on bald tires
weave like a breeze
through the traffic
on Marcus Avenue.

I am driving back
from Office Depot
with some paper stock
for printing business cards,
ten to a page.
Avery calls it *Clean Edge*,
no messy perforations.

Their motorcycles
cross three lanes
to make a sudden left.
How easily the pieces
can be torn apart.

Meditation on Picasso's *Old Guitarist*

Did you fall asleep,
listening to your own lullaby,
or did you die of hunger
waiting for a grateful audience?
Behind you stands a wall
as old and shabby as yourself.

Where are the coins
around your naked feet?
How long will this guitar,
your only wealth,
remain securely in your arms
before an opportunist rogue
purloins it for a handful of pesetas?

Will your sons, estranged,
be shamed to learn your fate?
Will their eyes grow wet,
their throats constrict
some years from now
hearing across the plaza
a familiar mournful tune
first learned from you?

And will they think
how once you cradled them
as gently as your sweet guitar
and strummed their little hearts
with tender, virtuoso hands?

DIE BEFORE YOU DIE

> I was cheered
>   when I came first to know
> that there were flowers also
>   in hell.
>
> —William Carlos Williams, "Asphodel, That Greeny Flower"

> I felt a Funeral, in my Brain,
> And Mourners to and fro
> Kept treading—treading—till it seemed
> That Sense was breaking through—
>
> —Emily Dickinson #280

Accelerating

This on-ramp is short,
meeting the highway
at the base of a steep hill.
My old four-cylinder Toyota
struggles with the climb,
recently more hesitant and slow.

Sometimes I observe
the impatience of a Lexus
looming right behind me,
sometimes simply my own dread
of what approaches imperceptibly.

Throwing It All Out

I look forward to the mail arriving—
a difficult habit to break,
like watching waves tumble onto shore,
though waves usually know where to stop,
and the moon pulls them out to sea again.

I wait for waves of mail that never stop
and most of which I toss in the recycle bin.
The rest I distribute around the house,
my wife's share on the sideboard,
some by the computer and checkbook,
magazines on a table by the front door
to read on the elliptical training machine
at the gym.

Whatever I don't throw out today
must be discarded later:
newspapers and catalogs, cardboard packaging,
books uninspected since purchase,
eight cabinets of files, and not only paper—
a spare tire from some previous car,
expired medications, an inherited bell collection,
unused wedding gifts of silver plate and demitasse,
business suits of a younger, thinner man,
all pending disposition.

And that is just the beginning.
Coin collection, art collection, recorded music,

poetry books, more than fifty amaryllis plants,
stained glass windows and light fixtures,
a favorite leather chair and a Bokhara carpet,
all things of attachment, all in frequent use,
and so much more, all to be released.

Even the wife herself,
the dust she stops vacuuming after she dies,
as well as my own dust and the urn to hold it.

No moon can help with this.
Either we evacuate ourselves
or leave our rubbish to posterity.
It has taken sixty years to learn this
and may take an additional sixty
in one lifetime or another
to finish throwing everything out.

An intriguing fantasy returns:
moving van, packed with possessions,
pulls away from the curb and instantly
bursts into flames, a total loss.

Last Car

"This will be the last car,"
my mother would announce
at 65 and again at 70
and 75 years of age.
She had already lived longer
than either of her parents.

And I am starting
to think like she did.
I can hear it in my thoughts:
"I might wear out
before this comforter,
before the microwave oven."

She said it again
at 80 and 85
(on a long drive,
one knee would stiffen).
And I will be gone
before this coffee table.

Am I in a race with my
Toyota, this pair of shoes,
the wall to wall carpet?
Or does everything have
its own countdown
to impermanence?

And so, no race at all—
each one's decay
unique unto itself.
She said it again in her nineties,
at long last living up to
her expectations of mortality.

Daredevil

Whenever I descend the stairs
carrying something bulky with both hands,
unable to grasp the railing, I think,
*This could be it—the buckled knee,
cracked skull, and long wait for the corpse
to be discovered in an empty house.*

Such thoughts might spring from morbid fears
or even hidden wishes—though I doubt it,
knowing how danger tenderly alerts our frailty
in the daily march of necessary risk—

even wrings a triumph, something like the way
I wake in the morning, instantly pleased
that the house is not on fire, my limbs not paralyzed.

Fugaces Labuntur Anni[8]

My life insurance company
wants me to live forever,
but my own desire ends within a century,
and only that long if I am sound and spry.
Though birthdays stack like poker chips,
I'm still not old enough for spry.

I remember him—that youth—
when all he wanted was
your pelvic treasure, sunny Baja,
Gewürztraminer, Szechwan beef,
Mission Style stained glass,
a goose down comforter…

one long, sensational list
in a short, expired season.
Regret, accept, and laugh—
pondering the retrospect—
my ante in infinity.

Für Elyse

I was hungry, so I called
the Mexican take-out restaurant
around the corner, even though
sky was gathering its thunder.

As I requested lunch, she said,
"Oh, I know you!" and I relished
the caress of her recognition.
Her English is getting so much better,

I thought, but when I arrived
to pick up the food, she was someone
I had never seen before,
both of us embarrassed.

That morning Elyse had confided in
our little group about her brother's
sudden death, and every painful detail
trembled in me like a restive audience.

As I carried food back home,
a cool mist began to dab my face,
while sunbeams warmed
the back of my neck.

I glanced up at the sky—
half of it blue and white
like a tee shirt and faded jeans,
half gray as oil smoke.

I looked around for a rainbow,
but all by itself, without any rainbow,
this was a sky under which to linger
at once both sinister and bright.

Drivers on Lakeville Road
must have wondered,
What is he doing?
What is he looking for up there?

Wary of Unbearable Lightness

I am counting on gravity
to keep myself grounded—
indeed, the psychic ballast,
the ineluctable authority
of all the gravities:

A husky gravitas to guide
each detour from my customary paths,
those gravel tailings of my daily digs,
the gravitation of being to being,
and, yes—the graves.

I need them all
lest I hover in vacuous suspense,
a balloon character adrift,
plaything of erratic winds.

Asymptomatic Mortality

"My life will soon be finished,"
I acknowledge, explaining why
I didn't argue with her.

In the anteroom of death,
what would be the point
of an angry retort?

She eyes me closely,
drenched in the news,
solemn in agreement.

Relinquishing her own
annoyance, she ventures,
"What… are you dying of?"

"Nothing in particular.
Nothing just yet."

Lives to Spare

I open my eyes—and die,
put on my bathrobe, pass away,
walk into the kitchen and expire.

Eating oatmeal
I come to an end.
While showering I perish.

As I put on my shoes
I depart this life.
Starting the car,

I give up the ghost.
And so it goes—such
is the prowess of death.

And so I, too, go on,
but more as verbs
than pronoun.

Perish the Thought

"Die before you die, and you will never die."
This Sufi maxim I remember, but not the names
of dead and buried selves:
bits of foreign languages once memorized,
algebra and physics formulas,
every revelation I had that night
on the truth serum of mescaline,
Kennedy cabinet officers, the capital of Indiana,
names of characters in *Measure for Measure*,
what I gave or received on various birthdays,
poetic waves that crested in the mind
and fell in the next instant, forever lost,
entire years from which
not one clear memory survives,
hundreds of titles on bookshelves,
and the whereabouts of countless items
in the household inventory.

Now, approaching decade number eight,
memory in steeper decline,
shall I welcome these accelerated deaths
as proof of immortality?
"Die before you die, and you will never die."
And there they go again:
expiring like isolated snowflakes
recycled into other places, other lives.
Death is mostly this reciprocal exchange,
withdrawing light from here
as it ignites a different chandelier.

Sonnet for Thich Nhat Hanh

As all fine words, with use, approach cliché
and settled living risks an empty rite,
only students of the agonies can say
what wakes a heart's inertia to the light.
Not cool serenity from Chardonnay,
nor coffee's surge to mindful energy.
But, as each crisis clarifies the way,
the suffered moment wrings a change in me.
Supine in my absurd Geworfenheit
I might object to being grounded here
until I learn to pose the question right:
Where would I be without the earth so near?
Content, I ride the current of this breath.
A lotus opens on the pond of death.

Mortality Through the Seasons

I

Puckering their lips
in briefest courtship,
sprightly daffodils bend to kiss
the perfumed hyacinths,
whistle overtures to spring.
Crocus and tulip stand and wither,
iris and lily wave and disappear.
This glad indifference of the flower
astonishes the always dying hour.

In spring, life seems to lengthen
with the swelling day.
Anticipation shivers in the dawn;
the fervid grass perspires.
But night that falls
throughout the year
arouses one recurrent fear:
flowers into darkness,
darkness in the flowers.

II

Velvet summer staggers
in the dripping heat,
a short time in a long life.
Languid labors are

distracted, incomplete.
Every moment falls away unfinished—
friends, careers, and loves
buried in their youth.
Here and there a wise word ripens,
a few ideas mature to harvest
while grass so soon turns brown.

Not far off, the fall of leaves
that will repeat
the fall of petals, fall of flakes.
Impossible, insistent cravings
bully the idle holidays.
Memories ribboned in regret
penetrate the soporific haze.
Unfamiliar paths or rutted circles
cannot point the way as time recedes
and sluggish waves with no intent
stumble to the stony beach.

III

Leaves release their grip
as if a plague had struck;
alarming numbers fall.
By long and irreversible tradition,
the glum accountancy of death
closes profit out with loss.

Their afterlife is full of color
like the blood of martyrs

or the flaming of a funeral pyre.
The blood we glimpse in such a season
shows death and life a sanguine reason.

Late in the old man's grayest age
I carried dahlias from the yard.
His rheumy eyes grew bright
as he remembered blooms
from sixty years before.
We spoke of dahlias
like two theologians.

A growing company of ghosts
attends my raking meditation in the yard
They linger here with me,
and I open to them,
two worlds resolving into one—
scattered, desiccated beings
ending in this universal heap,
as grief gapes into death.

IV

Unexpected snowflakes
gambol from the heights.
Trees encircled tremble, limbs aloft
in speechless, soft surrender.
Gallant paratroopers, all in white,
tumble over field and street.
The sky's invasion is complete.

Watching from the steps, I, too, am frozen.
Then—even the wind is breathless,
dies. Courtly stillness overtakes
the flow of every living thing.
A few last flakes glide to rest,
and in the overwhelming hush
this generosity of white converts
the heaviness of earth to light.

What my shovel scoops
already has been melting.
The sun, our ruddy neighbor
up the way, flashes a celestial smile.
Children at the corner shriek
and scramble over trails
freshly pressed into the snowscape.
Above their instant world
gray brightens into blue.

Their joy ignites my own,
replenishes the vanished years,
prepares me for another turn.
Spring is peering through this storm
as dawn stares into night,
as flesh envisions soul.

POISED TO EVAPORATE

It's only oblivion, true:
We had it before, but then it was going to end.
    —Philip Larkin, "The Old Fools"

Heroes of the Holocene

Salvia: flowering plant in the mint family.

Archeologists call them Natufians,
the first people known to practice burial rites.
They lined their graves with salvia.

Fourteen thousand years ago
near present-day Mt. Carmel—
long before Hades and Persephone,
before Anubis and Osiris,
before Yahweh and Lucifer—
they lined their graves with salvia,
imagining an after-breath of soul.

Rare is the person who has heard of
Natufians, civilization's pioneers,
slicing stalks of rye at Tell Abu Hureyra
with the earliest sickle blades.
They settled long enough to establish
agriculture in the middle east,
invented bread and beer.
They dug to plant their crops and
dug fresh graves they lined with salvia.

Natufians carved jewelry from bones,
chiseled limestone idols in lusty embrace.
The skeletal remains reveal
that more than half their offspring
perished during childhood.

Founders of Jericho, Natufians
fished in the Jordan River,
hunted gazelles, domesticated canines.

These heroes of the Holocene
flourished for millennia, far longer
than the Pax Romana or the Renaissance.

With kisses and tears they tucked
their children into beds of salvia.

Late-Stage American Hegemony

"Politicians are a lagging indicator."
    —Bill McKibbon

Young hippies who rebelled
by getting high, growing wild hair,
and levitating the Pentagon
are in their seventies now—
gray-haired grandparents
hoping the Establishment
will survive long enough
to send them twenty-five years
of retirement income.

I know— I'm one of them.
I sent LBJ a Mother's Day card
in 1968 that said,
"Happy Mother's Day, you mother!"
The FBI is probably still
interviewing my neighbors.

Hey, hey, LBJ!
How many kids
did you kill today?

Ho, Ho, Ho Chi Minh!
The Viet Cong
is gonna win!

My friend Louie joined the SDS,
more radical than I.
He banged his head against the war.
Oh, Janet (wherever you are),
do you remember
your bloodied boyfriend, Louie?
Do you remember me
organizing a peace demonstration
by the squirrels on campus?

Johnson seems less evil now,
Vietnam offset by Medicare and civil rights.
Most of his successors remind me
more of Nero than Augustus.
I've had a long time to watch
as everything that could have been
free, happy, safe, and true
was sprayed with Agent Orange,
fattened with corn syrup,
deceived by artificial intelligence,
or folded into collateralized obligations
for sale to the unsuspecting.

Some believe in progress,
others in a lumbering pendulum that swings
between prosperity and want, peace and war.
The darkest minds observe no more
than rolling ignorance without agenda,
disguised at times by luck and vagary.
But always, history echoes and ricochets.

The barbarians loom at Gate 57,
though our genocide is mainly self-inflicted.
The ghost of Edward Gibbon,
from his quiet resting place
in Fletching, Sussex,
has seen this all before.

You Don't Need a Weatherman

Tuesday's forecast: mostly sunny
with temperatures in the mid-70s,
ten percent chance of rain.
Tuesday evening,
shortly before midnight,
the large meteor Caligula
will crash into Earth
near Hibbing, Minnesota,
an impact equivalent
to eight hundred thousand
gigantic nuclear warheads,
throwing billions of tons
of debris into the air,
where it will block out sunlight
for hundreds of years and
extinguish nearly all forms of life.

Wednesday will be hazy and cooler,
with temperatures dropping
to the low 50s.

Subject to Change Without Notice

It was drafty at home
when all the doors disappeared.
I didn't mind the missing steeples,
stop signs, Styrofoam, student loans,
war zones, end zones, calzones.
Vanished: boons, banes, and bugaboos,
the complete works of Fill-in-the-Blank,
several stages of grief.
I hardly noticed when all the Bureau Chiefs
went out to lunch, never to return.

Soon there was not a monad or syllogism
left anywhere on the planet,
no double takes, clam bakes, spring breaks,
no B. S., no P. S., no T. S. Eliot,
no hollow men or ragged claws,
neither a bang nor a whimper
amid the plunging decrescendo
of favorite symphonies. I looked in vain
for fast balls, fast cars, fast food,
grandes dames, blame games, street names.
I would have asked the few remaining
carpenters for new doors, but by then
housing had imploded.

I didn't miss
paper money, papier mâché, pay per view,
pratfalls, pitfalls, windfalls, cat calls.

Everyone's Going

I knew only a few of all the people
once named Flynn and Gonzalez.
No dreadlocks, headlocks, wedlocks.
Where are they now—the secret handshakes
and gentlemen's agreements,
boycotts, tomboys, home boys, choir boys,
boy toys, game boys, killjoys?

Sparrows hopping in the snow disappeared,
then every type of winged and feathered aviator
that once had nested in the former trees.
Things stopped slipping through my fingers
once I lost my fingers.

Panic flared concurrent with the latest plague,
a persistent duo of contagion
until these, likewise, withdrew
along with ragtime, tea time, half time, bedtime,
one or more Persons of the Trinity
(the exact number not disclosed),
and everything sweet except love—
then even your embrace.

The end of glaciers had been foretold,
but not the pale voids
where primary colors once gleamed,
not the faltering grip of gravity,
time's drastic tachycardia.
History vanished in a noisy gulp,
like a treasure-laden galleon

into the Devil's Triangle.
A billion stars winked shut, mere sparks
in dark recesses of a frigid universe.

The infinite surplus of future events,
the inexhaustible spare change of kinetic energy
funnel down to a last drop of dew
poised to evaporate beneath a missing sunrise.

Endnotes

1 "I still can't see very far into suffering," translated by Cliff Crego.

2 "They harvest the wine of their eyes," first line of *Die Winzer* by Paul Celan.

3 "Hit the bull's eye." Literally, "Hit into the black."

4 "The preciousness of sentient life and the nearness of death."

5 Translated by Claire Louise Harmon, *Poetry*, May 2022 p. 143.

6 "To the stars through difficulties." Motto of Kansas, her birthplace.

7 Literally, "free sea." 1. A navigable body of water open to all nations. 2. Freedom of the seas.

8 Horace, "The fleeting years slip away."

Acknowledgments

All the Men Came and Danced (anthology): "Awaiting Flowers," "With This Ring"

Bards' Annual (anthology): "Chair by the Window," "Decision," "Subject to Change Without Notice"

Brevitas (anthology): "Asymptomatic Mortality"

Buddhist Poetry Review, "Extended Memory"

Freshet, "Christmas Mourning," "Even an Attractive Cage," "Für Elyse," "Good Friday in the Sky," "Planting Fields Arboretum, Followed by Lunch," "Return Trip"

Generations, "Last Car"

Halfway Down the Stairs, "Death Benefit"

Long Island Quarterly, "Bedside Manners"

Long Island Sounds, "Memorial Day"

Moon Magazine, "Last Haircut," "Late-Stage American Hegemony," "Lives to Spare," "Perish the Thought"

Nassau County Poet Laureate Review, "Dorothy's Last Year," "In the Woman Cave"

New York State Psychologist, "Making It Official"

Oberon, "Atlantic Waves," "Heroes of the Holocene"

Performance Poets Association Literary Review, "A Soft Retirement," "One Death, a Threnody," "Sonnet for Thich Nhat Hanh," "Your 98th Birthday"

Poetry Frog, "Into Pieces"

Sprout, "Little Wooden Things"

The Whirlwind Review, "Wary of Unbearable Lightness"

About Atmosphere Press

Founded in 2015, Atmosphere Press was built on the principles of Honesty, Transparency, Professionalism, Kindness, and Making Your Book Awesome. As an ethical and author-friendly hybrid press, we stay true to that founding mission today.

If you're a reader, enter our giveaway for a free book here:

SCAN TO ENTER
BOOK GIVEAWAY

If you're a writer, submit your manuscript for consideration here:

SCAN TO SUBMIT
MANUSCRIPT

And always feel free to visit Atmosphere Press and our authors online at atmospherepress.com. See you there soon!

About the Author

GEORGE H NORTHRUP is a poet and psychologist in New Hyde Park, New York. He was President of the Fresh Meadows Poets from 2006 to 2024 and served on the Board of the Nassau County Poet Laureate Society. *Everyone's Going* is his fifth poetry collection.

Northrup was President of the New York State Psychological Association in 2009 and a member of the Council of Representatives that governs the American Psychological Association from 2012 through 2014.

www.ingramcontent.com/pod-product-compliance
Lightning Source LLC
LaVergne TN
LVHW041621070526
838199LV00052B/3211